Miss I Know Everything

Emil Claire

BookLeaf Publishing
India | USA | UK

Presentation by *BookLeaf Publishing*

Web: www.bookleafpub.com

E-mail: info@bookleafpub.com

ISBN: 9789363318762

First edition 2024

To mini-er(?) claire,

keep reading kid, it works out in the end.

ACKNOWLEDGEMENTS

I'd like to thank (for the second time hee hee) myself for somehow being able to continue writing. None of us thought you could do it again, so imagine how shocked we are.

A special shout-out to my only child, Bean Claire. I forgot him last time. He is the world's most energetic and bubbly dog.

This collection was inspired by a lot of different media and is, in a way, a love letter to the art that helped me with my work.

So, without further ado…flip the page. Also, please fall in love with and obsess over my writing. Thank you.

Part I:

my teenage diorama

out of the blue

Sitting on the tiles,
fighting a little smile
sunlight on her face,
a windy embrace.

On entering home,
she wrote a poem
it was all her own,
she did not feel alone.

grandfather clock

2

To the little girl who couldn't sleep,
you dream beautiful dreams
The little mind that always thought,
the silences are serene
The little body who never felt like enough,
you are cherished beyond compare

You are no longer little and with it no longer
brittle.

self-love for a sunday

3

I hate my face because it stares,
my hair because its everywhere,
my skin because it's full of pores,
and my knees keep hitting doors,
my lips are always cracking,
my tummy's nonstop snacking,
I hate my thighs because it's like jelly,
why are my armpits so darn smelly?
my feet because they're enormous,
my hands are simply the coldest
I hate myself mostly because I'm there.

tea party

I sit at the table but I'm not really there
listen to their fable but don't really care
try not to enable, they think nothing's fair
nod as if it's fatal, they are everywhere
drink till I'm able, I'd rather be anywhere

the white daffodil

5

Stolen glances that were rare
I moved on but you stayed there
never even knowing that you cared
Now I see your name pass by
whispers of a 'You and I'
is all that we can now share
Maybe in a little time
the past will heal and we'll just smile
it was all by fate's design
You'll find someone good enough
I'll just turn into some fluff
from a past that won't compare
Know that I'll be wonderstruck
memories in written muck
and that'd you stay right there

that girl

I wish I was one of the girls
always somewhere fun
doing something dumb
feeling rich and young
being pretty and loved

heart-shaped sunglasses

Should I buy it, should I not
silent echoes tie a knot
feel my morals leave
It's so shiny, it's so hot
it'll make what you're not
you can play make believe
Mind is reeling, you feel caught
it's just fabric but you forgot
there's no sense of relieve

arson baby

8

I feel like burning something
the house needs the color
it would be that dumb thing
that made my life less duller

matilda

9

we didn't have to be friends
(you could've just pretend)
we could've just played
(but you never stayed)
we should've just talked
(but you always fought)
I guess you won the game
(now you're just a name)

kindred spirits

do you feel it in the air?
just how much we cared
that last summer
the breeze was in my hair
fruit sandwiches we shared
that last summer
watching movies in the chair
you had come prepared
that last summer
I hope you know it wasn't fair
I was always scared
of our last summer

golden compass

Your eyes lit up when you saw the rain
said it reminded you of times
you wish you could maintain.
Old school days that flew
away like a paper plane
You sigh and smile as you kindly explain
that life is just a 'silly little train'.
Well I hope you're happy and
I hope you left all the pain
Cause I know that all of it is hard to maintain
but none of it was done in vain.
You are someone words can't contain
so I'll pray that you're still just as mundane
with your softness and snores
and quiet refrain
and the next time it rains
I hope you know that
I have nothing to complain.

bunny

i suck all the time
it's so bad i even rhyme
you'd think i'm just being dramatic
but everything i do is erratic
i am terrible at basic stuff
even being nice is really tough
pretty sure i'm the problem child
but wouldn't it be boring if I was mild?
i feel kinda narcissistic
but if we're being real i'm just pessimistic
so damn loud and so annoying
god you're just so disappointing
feeling sad? of course you do
your favorite color is literally blue
stop writing this poem and get some medication
the doctor's tip? 'go on a vacation'

vengeance

13

mom found some snails, slugs
and slimy little thugs
so I have to deal with the bugs
while the angel says oh so smug
'that's the hole that you dug'
while giving me a nonchalant shrug
so I'm just gonna pull under the rug
and give her the sweetest little hug
because she'd never guess what's in her mug

tomb raider

I like digging graves
along with pearly ghosts
we charter dingy boats
and act really depraved
we bid a solemn farewell
as I banish them to the hotel
and walk my way back to the house

maneater

15

I might kill all men
my curfew's up till ten
it's not like any of them are a Ken.

would it be funny if I did it with a pen?

cherry lips

I tell you a secret
you tell me four
show you my trinkets
are we something more?
avoid me in the hallways
guess I'm now a bore
the rumors are spreading
I stare at the floor
show up at my house
I leave you at the door
"I would never do that!"
that's what you swore
you're just a psycho
and I'm just a score

sugar plum

Can I just live in the clouds?
it would be so fluffy and calm
and I doubt I would be in any harm
and maybe I could start a farm
with cotton candy crowds

soliloquy

It would be nice
if I could just cry
and not have to try
to pretend like I'm not angry
It would be nice
to start a conversation
without an interpretation
of why my body looks how does
It would be nice
to just like what I like
not go on a mental strike
on account of gender politics
It would be nice
to be treated with respect
and not need to suspect
every person I meet
It would be nice
if we didn't hold on to 1950's morals
and stopped having stupid quarrels
and just did what we wanted
there's a lot of other things that would be nice
but it's not like my opinion matters
and I don't see the glass ceiling in tatters
so I guess it'll just stay "nice"

stargazer

do you see the skies
where the heavenly body lies
the constellations and stars
from saturn to mars
and how the planets align
to form all those signs
and all that we learn
just makes a child yearn
to travel to space
and explore that shifty place

2007 (retrograde version)

everything feels different
from than it once did
maybe it's just nostalgia
or maybe it's just being a kid
film looks clearer and
the clothes are changing
everyone looks inconsistent
like their faces are rearranging
there are new terms every day
the internet is submerging
people create their own personas
maybe society is self-purging?
people make everything into politics
it's suffocating me
the literal world is burning
just let others be
so many new things are happening
we might be in a sci-fi movie
everything sucks so the end
of the world could be groovy
it's easy to lose faith in humanity
because we're acting like a circus
I'm not sure what the joke is
but it's definitely not on purpose

heretic

"Why would Satan punish sinners?
After all, they are his winners"
The priest merely smiled and
looked into the other's eyes
"Have you come here once again,
to undo at my cant?"
For I too can point at a tree and say,
'was this not once a plant?'
"Don't you think it be easier father,
had I not been such a bother?"
"Had we not had our quarrels,
I would not be as secure in my morals."
The man looks quite pleased,
as though the day had been seized.
"Are you staying for the mass?"
"No, I think I'll pass."

girl failure

I'm not ambitious and I'm not smart
all I have are really bad marks
I would rather hibernate in a cave
than actually do something quite brave
I suck at most of the things I do
and don't see others saying "me too!"
I'm mostly sad than happy
most people would probably call me crappy
I'm selfish and not at all aphoristic
more like terrible and extremely masochistic
I would never be a boss
sometimes I think I look like moss
By societal standards I'd be a disappointment
and that's the kind of pain that has no ointment
I don't think I'll be successful in terms of money
but hey at least I'll still be somewhat funny
I have horrible taste in music and fashion
what's the point of having passion?
And I should definitely get therapy
but I prefer acting like there's nothing with me
In case it's hard to tell from my behavior,
I feel like a dumb girl failure
And I just wish I could die
cool, now I'm gonna go cry

print society

I don't like social media.
It feels like someone's trying
to stuff in an encyclopedia
full of information but
it's not useful and
I don't need it.

heart skips

24

I heard that when you sneeze,
your heart stops for a second
Why did my heart
not continue stopping?

butterfly away

Someday I'll move on
to bigger things
with better dreams
Someday I'll move on
to different seasons
and walkable views
Someday I'll move on
to find my people
and find myself
Someday I'll move on
to a happier life
and feel content
Someday I'll move on
to do what I like
and hate what I like
for now I'll have days
like today
until I make my way

enchanted

I want to be in a field
filled with beautiful flowers
whose names I will not remember
with the sun shining,
but not too brightly
to feel the heat
clouds present
and an ever-so chilly breeze
not hot enough to feel warm
not cold enough to shiver
the ground not dirty enough
to harm my clothes
but just enough to dust off
with tiny lovely beings who bother none
and just exist
somewhere I am just a small creature
where I am nothing
and do nothing
merely a small dot
appreciating a
bigger and wilder dot

fin

I have never been good at saying goodbye.
But I have learned that when somethings ends,
it does not mean it's gone forever
It merely means that something else can begin
Nothing truly leaves because memory keeps it
alive
So, I'm not saying goodbye
because as long as I remember,
you never really left.

vanity

You cannot let someone
into your home
if you do not live in it
your self

loquacious

29

Someone who grew up loud and rambunctious
told that they found stillness uncomfortable
was shocked to find that quiet brought calm
and all the words uttered could never reach the
warmth
that they found was there all along.

poser

I can smile and I can talk
make compliments and take a walk
be polite and not just gawk
Back-handed comments I can shake
most events feel a mistake
but why do I feel so fake?
Everyone seems to fit in
I keep wondering how long it's been
it's getting under my skin
Fix my posture, brush it off
break right in with a cough
I tell myself it's a one-off
This clearly not who you are
should we just bolt, get in the car?
I feel so bizarre

Part II:

the poet by the pond: lilypad sessions

a tune for the blues

33

grief is not anger or sadness or sorrow
it's the all the love and care you have left
it's all the unaddressed letters in your room
all the words you never spoke out loud
it is not a dark and gloomy thing
though it is born out of loss
it is the most sincere and
bare form of love
which is why
it hurts
all so
much

silly goose

34

I hit my ankle on the door
it can't be undone
I walked down the stairs
the cat watched as I spun
I tried to laugh it off
and made a bad pun
I wanted to make pancakes
but how much is a ton?
I needed some yarn to knit
but now there was none
I feel positively jinxed
though the day has just begun
I don't think being a silly goose
is quite all that fun

wonderland

There were benches to sit
to watch the ducks waddle
and the frogs croak.
Peer down as the lilies float,
swirling softly as they create ripples
in the blue pocket pond.
The daffodils looked as yolk-yellow
as the ducklings in the water.
Pollen drifting like pixie dust
as the sun washes the area
with its golden glow.
The trees overflowing with
blushing pink blossoms.
There was that glimpse
of eternal peace.

Cat

Outside my house, lives a cat
in a corner by the tree, it sat
I fed it well but found no fat
in fact, for a cat it was very flat
Winter was chill so I made it a hat
it looked quite pleased by that
The cat was definitely no brat
it actually was friends with the rat
We always have a lovely chat
sipping my tea with her by the mat

Part III:

castle walls

XOXO

39

If you ever feel stupid
about something you're doing
say, writing a poem,
just remember people do
silly things all the time.
So, write your little heart out
because I'm sure it'll be sublime.